BARN OWLS

BARN OWLS

by Wolfgang Epple/photographs by Manfred Rogl

A Carolrhoda Nature Watch Book

Carolrhoda Books, Inc./Minneapolis

Thanks to Dr. Gary Duke of The Raptor Center at the University of Minnesota for his assistance with this book.

This edition first published 1992 by Carolrhoda Books, Inc.
Original edition copyright © 1988 by Kinderbuchverlag Reich Luzern AG, Lucerne, Switzerland, under the title DIE SCHLEIEREULE. Translated from the German by Amy Gelman.
Adapted by Carolrhoda Books, Inc.
All additional material supplied for this edition © 1992 by Carolrhoda Books, Inc.

LIBRARY OF CONGRESS CATALOGING-IN-PUBLICATION DATA

Epple, Wolfgang
    [Schleiereule. English]
    Barn owls / by Wolfgang Epple : photographs by Manfred Rogl
      p.   cm.
    Translation of: Die Schleiereule
    "A Carolrhoda nature watch book"
    Includes index.
    Summary: Describes the physical characteristics, habitat, and life cycle of the barn owl.
    ISBN: 0-87614-742-2
    1. Barn owl—Juvenile literature. [1. Barn owl. 2. Owls.]
I. Rogl, Manfred, ill. II. Title.
QL696.S85E6613   1992
598′.97—dc20   91-36818
                                   CIP
                                   AC

Manufactured in the United States of America

1 2 3 4 5 6 97 96 95 94 93 92

It is a moonlit night in early spring. The houses of the small country village are dark. All the people have gone to sleep. Then through the quiet night comes a hoarse cry that causes the sleepers to stir in their beds. *Croooh-croooh! Croooh-croooh!*

If you looked up into the night sky, you might be able to see the creature that is producing this eerie sound. It is a barn owl flying over the sleeping village. The white underside of the owl's body gleams in the moonlight. Its wide wings flutter like the wings of a large moth. Circling slowly, the barn owl gives its strange call again and again. *Croooh-croooh! Croooh-croooh!*

The great horned owl lives in dense forests in the northern and eastern regions of the United States.

Not many people are lucky enough to see a barn owl gliding through the night sky. Yet barn owls are common birds in many regions of the world. They are the most widespread of all owls, found in parts of North, Central, and South America, as well as Europe, Asia, Africa, and Australia.

Many of the world's owls, for example, the great gray owl, live in remote forests or in other places far from people's homes. The barn owl is different. This bird is often found in areas inhabited by humans.

If barn owls have a choice, they prefer to make nests in hollow trees or holes in cliffs. But they also live in barns, churches, grain elevators, old houses, and other deserted buildings. They can be found in cities and towns as well as in rural areas. But because barn owls are active only at night, people usually don't realize that they have owls for neighbors.

The barn owl was given its common name because of its habit of living in people's barns. Its scientific name, *Tyto alba*, is based on its appearance. *Tyto* is a Greek word meaning "owl." *Alba* is Latin for "white" and refers to the beautiful white feathers on the underside of a barn owl's body.

The barn owl has some other names that also come from the way it looks. Sometimes people call it the monkey owl. With its long legs, dark eyes, and heart-shaped face, a barn owl does looks something like a small monkey with feathers. But it is definitely a bird — a very special kind of bird.

In this book, you will meet some real barn owls and find out just what makes them so special.

The barn owls shown in this book live near a small village in Europe (opposite). This village has not changed much in hundreds of years. It is made up of a cluster of farms where people raise chickens and cows and grow vegetables in garden plots. Surrounding the village are orchards, grassy meadows, and woody thickets. A stream bordered by alder trees wanders nearby.

This village has many good homes for barn owls. The church has a tall bell tower that is open on the sides. Many of the barns, sheds, and other farm buildings in the area have small windows in their upper stories. People leave these windows open so that barn owls can come inside. They are glad to have the birds living around their farms.

The photographs in this book were taken inside one of these barns (above), where a family of owls has made a home.

9

A male barn owl (above) was the first to go in through the owl window in the barn. He inspected the barn loft and saw that it would be a good place to raise a family. Now he had to find a mate.

To attract a female, the male owl flew above the village, making his mating call (right). *Croooh-croooh*. This hoarse, rasping cry isn't very pleasant to human ears, but female barn owls find it appealing. A female in the area heard this male's call and came to check him out as a possible mate.

The two owls flew to the barn, and the male went into the loft. He called loudly to the female and stamped his feet on the ground. He was showing her the great place that he had selected to raise a family. But the female still needed to be convinced that the male would make a good mate and a good father to their young.

A pair of barn owls. The male (right) is smaller than the female.

11

One way that a male owl can win over a female is to bring her food (above). If the two owls have young, the male will have to play a big role in feeding the baby owls. He can show the female that he will be a good provider by presenting her with a mouse that he has caught.

That is just what the male barn owl did. After receiving a fat mouse as a "wedding present," the female accepted the male as her partner. During the next few days, the two owls mated many times (above). Then the female started laying the eggs from which their young would hatch.

Barn owls can lay as many as 10 or 11 eggs at a time, but they usually have only 3 to 6. The eggs are laid two or three days apart.

As soon as each egg appears, the female barn owl starts to **incubate (IN-kew-bate)** it. She sits on the egg and keeps it warm so that the chick inside can develop. Some other female birds start to incubate only after they have laid all their eggs.

The female in the barn loft has laid five eggs (above). She keeps them tucked under her, warm and safe against her **brood spot**, a featherless area on her breast. Every 20 minutes or so, the female stands up and gently rearranges the eggs with her beak and the stiff

14

feathers on her face (below). By doing this, she makes sure that all the eggs receive the same amount of warmth during incubation.

What is the male barn owl doing while his mate is busy tending the eggs? Unlike some other male birds, he does not share in the work of incubation. His job is to feed his mate during this important period. He proves to be a good partner, bringing mice, voles, and other small mammals to the female every day.

After the eggs have been incubated for about 28 days, they begin to hatch. As you might expect, the egg that was laid first is the first one to hatch. Every two to three days, another owl chick breaks out of its egg. By the time the last egg hatches, the first chick will already be two weeks old.

When an egg is ready to hatch, the chick inside begins cheeping softly. Before long, a hole appears in the egg shell (above). Working from the inside, the little owl gradually makes the hole larger (center). It may take several hours for the chick to cut its way out of the shell (below). Sometimes the mother owl helps by nibbling at the shell with her beak.

Like many young birds, the owl chick uses a special tool called an **egg tooth** to break open the shell. It is not actually a tooth—birds do not have teeth—but a kind of bump on its beak (indicated by arrow opposite). After the chick has hatched, the egg tooth will fall off.

When a little owl finally tumbles out into the world, it is very tired and weak. A newly hatched barn owl weighs only ¾ ounce (20 grams). Its eyes are closed, and its body is covered with a thin coat of down. The little animal depends completely on its parents for warmth, food, and protection.

Parent owls work very hard taking care of their young. A mother barn owl will defend her chicks fiercely from anything that might threaten them. If a person or an animal enters the barn and comes near the nest, the female owl becomes very upset. She spreads her wings and ruffles her feathers so that she looks larger (above). The owl also clicks her beak and makes hissing noises.

This display is meant to scare away the intruder. If it doesn't work, the female owl might attack with her strong, sharp claws. She will do anything she can to protect her helpless young.

Another important job of the mother owl is keeping the chicks warm. Their thin covering of downy feathers is not enough to protect them from the cold. During the first two weeks of their lives, the little owls spend most of their time huddled under the female's body (below). Here they are kept warm by her brood spot and by the soft feathers on her breast.

In addition to warmth, what the baby owls need most now is food. In order to grow into healthy adult barn owls, they must have a *lot* of food. Supplying it is the parents' biggest job.

Barn owls, like all their relatives, are strictly meat-eaters. Their nourishment comes from the flesh of mice (above), rats, voles, moles, and other small animals. Like eagles, hawks, and other **birds of prey**, owls get their food by hunting. And they are great hunters.

Every night at dusk, the male barn owl goes out to find food for his five hungry chicks. He flies low over the fields around the village, using his eyes and ears to locate prey.

The barn owl's eyesight is excellent. Like all owls, he can see well in both dim and bright light. But when hunting at night, he usually depends on his sharp hearing to catch prey.

The faintest rustling sound made by a mouse moving through dry leaves reaches the barn owl's ears. Quick as a flash, he adjusts his position until the sound is equal in both ears. Then, flapping his wide wings, he plunges head down toward the prey.

Just as he is about to reach the mouse, the owl raises his head and wings and swings his feet forward. He strikes the animal with his powerful **talons (TAL-uhns)**, or claws, and kills it instantly. Carrying the mouse in his beak, the male owl flies home to his family.

A barn owl uses its sharp hearing to track a mouse rustling through dry leaves.
The animal will provide food for the owl's hungry chicks.

While the male has been hunting, the female barn owl has been with the chicks. They are only a few days old and cannot be left alone for a minute. Now the male has arrived with dinner (left), and the female can feed her babies.

Adult owls usually swallow prey animals whole, gulping them down head first. But baby owls are too small and weak to eat in this way. So the female tears up the mouse with her beak. Then she makes a soft clucking sound to tell the chicks it is time to eat. The babies answer with a snorting noise. They open their mouths, and the mother owl feeds each of them small pieces of mouse (opposite).

While the female is feeding the young, the male goes out to find more food. Owl chicks need an enormous amount of food. The male has to supply at least 20 small animals a night to satisfy their hunger. He also has to catch prey for himself and his mate.

Now you can see why the male owl had to prove his hunting skill before the female would start a family with him. If he was not a good hunter, she and her young would simply not survive.

The male owl that lives in this barn is lucky. There are a lot of prey animals in the area around his village. The open fields and meadows hide many small, scurrying creatures. The owl can usually find food for his family.

When the weather is bad, however, hunting is not so easy. Rain causes many problems for the owl. If his soft feathers get wet, he cannot fly very well. But even worse, the rain makes it difficult for him to hear.

When mice and voles move through wet leaves, they do not make any noise. If the owl can't hear his prey, it is hard for him to find the little animals in the dark night. Then he may hunt in vain.

But this owl *is* lucky. There are many

A barn owl hunting prey inside a barn

barns in his village with plenty of mice rustling through the hay. He can get into the barns through the owl windows. Even if there isn't a window, the owl can squeeze through openings that are only six inches (15 cm) wide.

In the darkest barn, the male owl can catch mice by listening for the sound they make. Even in bad weather, he can find food for his chicks.

But when the owl chicks are about two weeks old, the male can no longer do the job alone. The young birds are growing so fast that he cannot bring enough food to satisfy them. Now the female owl must also go out to hunt each night.

The male and female barn owl with their young. It is very unusual to see both parent owls with the chicks at the same time.

By the time all the owl chicks are at least two weeks old, they do not need their mother with them constantly. Their dark eyes are open, and their white down covering is thick and warm.

When the female owl is in the nest, the young owls still cuddle close to her (opposite). Both mother and young seem to enjoy the contact. When they are alone, the chicks huddle together, with the smallest ones on the inside.

Every day at dusk, the chicks begin making rasping noises to let their parents know it's time to eat. The five chicks take turns calling for food. When one stops, another one takes up the noise. The adult owls get the message, and both fly out to start the night's hunt.

When one of the parent owls returns to the barn with a mouse or vole, it calls to the young with a clucking sound. Snorting noisily, the chicks rush to be fed. Usually the hungriest chick makes the most noise and pushes ahead of the others. This is the one that will get the prey (below).

By the time they are two weeks old, the young owls don't need to have their food torn up for them. Like adult owls, they can swallow prey animals whole

(left). Sometimes it takes a while for a chick to get a large animal down. The bird in the photograph on the right has swallowed everything but the tail.

Owls swallow their meals whole, but they cannot digest the bones, hair, and claws of a prey animal. Inside the owl's stomach, these leftover parts are formed into balls called **pellets** (below). The owl brings up the pellets from its stomach and spits them out. Many pellets can be found around places where owls nest or roost. Scientists often study them to find out what the birds are eating.

After swallowing an animal whole, an owl spits up pellets of hair and bones. The bird cannot digest these parts of a prey's body.

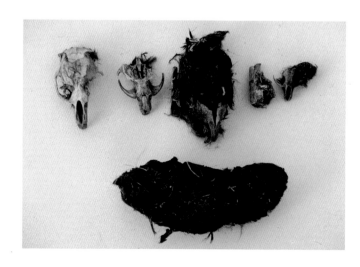

29

If food is plentiful, all the five chicks in the owl family will get enough to eat. When food is scarce, however, it is a different story. Then the biggest and strongest of the young owls get most of the food. These are usually the older chicks, like the two on the far left and right in the photograph above.

The younger birds are often too small and weak to fight for their share of food. Without enough to eat, these youngsters will eventually die. But if food had to be divided equally among all the chicks, then none might live.

Sometimes the chicks that die are even eaten by their older brothers and sisters. This is another way of making sure that at least some of the young owls will survive.

The owls growing up in this barn don't have to worry about not getting enough to eat. Their parents bring them plenty of food, and the five chicks continue to grow. By the time they are 17 days old, they can stand on their feather-covered legs. A few days later, they are walking around and even trying to flap their wings.

31

As the young owls continue to develop, their adult feathers begin to appear. They gradually replace the soft white down that the chicks are still wearing.

The stiff feathers on the chicks' faces are among the earliest to develop. These special feathers form what scientists call a **facial disk**. All owls have facial disks, but the barn owl's is particularly noticeable. It is shaped something like a heart.

An owl's facial disk seems to play an important role in hearing. The stiff feathers help to direct sound into the ears, which are located at the edge of the facial disk, behind the eyes.

Owls, like other birds, don't have the large external ears that many mammals have. An owl's ears are openings in its head surrounded by small flaps of skin. By moving these skin flaps and the feathers of the facial disk, a barn owl can pick up the faintest of sounds.

By the time the little owls are one month old, they already have the sharp hearing that they will use as hunters. Their eyesight is also well developed.

As the youngsters observe what is going on around them, they often turn and tilt their heads. This gives them a comical look, but they don't do it for fun. These movements are necessary for their vision.

An owl's eyes are fixed in their sockets. They cannot be moved freely as the eyes of many other animals can. In order to see something off to the side, an owl must turn its whole head. To see behind, owls turn their heads completely around to the back, first to one side and then the other. They can do this because they have very flexible bones in their necks.

Owls tilt their heads to one side to help in judging distance (above). By seeing an object from several different angles, an owl is better able to tell how far away it is. Head tilting is also useful in figuring out where sounds are coming from.

A young barn owl gets some exercise by running around the barn. When its wing feathers develop, it will take to the air.

Like all barn owls, the young owls fly in almost complete silence. This silent flight is made possible by the unusual structure of their wing feathers. The large **primary feather** that forms the leading edge of an owl's wing has a soft, downy fringe. This fringed edge reduces the sound made when the wing moves through the air.

Quiet flight makes it possible for a barn owl to hear the small sounds made by prey animals. It also allows the owl to swoop down on prey without warning.

A barn owl's first long wing feather has a soft fringed edge that reduces noise in flight.

At one month old, the little barn owls have become very active, especially at night. They jump on dead mice that their parents have brought, grasping them with their sharp little talons. Sometimes they try to catch flies with their beaks. They also use their beaks to groom each other's feathers.

The youngsters move around the barn a lot. They may spend hours "strolling," or they may suddenly start running back and forth (above). The oldest chicks are even beginning to fly. They now have most of their adult feathers (opposite), and they try out their newly developed wings by taking short flights within the barn.

By the time the young owls are about 35 to 40 days old, they have reached their adult weight. But their appetites remain enormous, and they eat as much as their parents will bring them.

At this stage, the parent owls weigh less than their young because they have been working so hard. They have to bring at least four field mice to each chick every night! If they don't catch enough prey one night, then they must make up the difference the following night.

Right now, the male owl is doing most of the work. He flies tirelessly back and forth, bringing food for his five hungry young (below). The female owl is not around much these days. She has left the young owls to the male's care so that she can start a second family.

The male and female owl have mated again, and the female is now ready to lay another set of eggs. Soon the male barn owl will have to collect even more food.

When the young owls are about two months old, they are all able to fly. But their hunting skills are not completely developed. They still need the help of their parents.

The five young owls have moved out of the barn into a big old pine tree nearby. Here they wait impatiently for their father to bring them food (above).

The male owl is really busy now. In between his trips to the old pine tree, he visits the bell tower of the church. Here his mate is incubating a new set of eggs. He must bring food to her as well as to his almost-grown young. No wonder he is sometimes in such a hurry that he lets go of a mouse before the young owls can grab it (right).

Barn owls can raise more than one family a year only in areas with long periods of warm, dry weather. Plenty of food must also be available. If prey animals are scarce, a male owl will not be able to feed two sets of young.

By the end of summer, the young owls raised in the barn can hunt for themselves. Now they are all living on their own. In the bell tower, their young brothers and sisters have just hatched out of their eggs. The male owl is still hunting throughout the night to feed his new family. It will be almost winter before the new chicks will be able to take care of themselves.

Barn owls have a hard time during cold, snowy winters. The mice and other small animals that they eat hide under snow. Owls can catch prey only if the snow is no more than three inches (8 cm) deep. In deeper snow, they cannot hear the animals and locate them.

During a long, hard winter, most of the barn owls in an area may die. The lucky ones may be able to get into barns or other buildings and find food there. Then they will be able to survive for one more year. Barn owls rarely live for more than 10 years. In the wild, their life span is usually only 2 to 3 years.

Barn owls are common in many parts of the world, but in some areas of the United States, they have almost disappeared. In midwestern states like Ohio, Illinois, Missouri, and Iowa, there are almost no barn owls left. What happened to these beautiful and useful birds?

Scientists believe that barn owls have disappeared in these areas because they no longer have enough to eat. Mice, voles, and other small prey animals usually live in meadows and grasslands. But they are not at home in large fields planted with neat rows of crops like corn and soybeans. And such fields are very common in many midwestern states.

Midwestern farmers are not happy that barn owls no longer live in their area. They know how useful the owls are in catching mice and other small animals that eat stored crops. But the birds will probably not return until their food supply returns.

If some midwestern grasslands could be left wild or used as meadows, then barn owls might have a chance. But people have to decide that the owls are worth giving up some land that could be planted with crops. Barn owls don't ask for much, but they must have enough food in order to survive.

GLOSSARY

birds of prey: owls, hawks, eagles, and other birds that get their food by hunting small animals

brood spot: a featherless area on an adult bird's breast used in incubating eggs. The warmth of the adult's body passes through the bare skin of the brood spot to the chicks inside the eggs.

egg tooth: a bump or projection on a chick's bill that is used to break open the egg shell. After the chick hatches, the egg tooth falls off.

facial disk: the ring of stiff feathers on an owl's face. The feathers of the facial disk can be moved in order to direct sounds into the owl's ears.

incubate: to keep eggs warm by sitting on them. Bird eggs must be incubated so that the young inside can complete their development.

pellets: small bundles or balls of hair and bones that owl spit up after eating. An owl's body cannot digest these hard parts of prey animals.

primary feather: one of the long flight feathers at the end of a bird's wing

talons: the strong, sharp claws of owls and other birds of prey

INDEX

ABOUT THE AUTHOR

Wolfgang Epple is a scientist and writer with a special interest in barn owls. He has studied these fascinating birds for many years. For his doctoral degree at the Max Planck Institute in Germany, he wrote a dissertation on the reproduction of barn owls. Wolfgang Epple now works for the Department of Wildlife Conservation in Stuttgart, Germany, where he helps to protect the future of barn owls and other wild creatures.

ABOUT THE PHOTOGRAPHER

Manfred Rogl has been a wildlife photographer for more than 20 years. His pictures have been widely published in books and magazines and have won many awards. To take the beautiful photographs in this book, he set up his camera in a barn loft where a pair of owls was raising a family. Manfred Rogl has also taken photographs for children's books about robins and woodpeckers. Born in Austria, he now makes his home in Switzerland.